Taking You Camera to AUSTRALIA

Ted Park

STECK-VAUGHN
ELEMENTARY · SECONDARY · ADULT · LIBRARY

A Harcourt Company

www.steck-vaughn.com

Printed and bound in the United States of America
10 9 8 7 6 5 4 3 2 1 W 04 03 02 01 00

Photo acknowledgments
Cover ©Ken Ross/FPG International; p.1 ©Superstock; p.3a ©Travelpix/FPG International;
p.3b ©Michaels, Christian/FPG International; p.3c ©VCG/FPG International; p.3d ©Patrick
Ward/CORBIS; p.4 ©Telegraph Colour Library/FPG International; pp.5, 8 ©Superstock; p.9
©Travelpix/FPG International; p.10 ©VCG/FPG International; p.12 ©Travelpix/FPG
International; p.13 ©Lloyd, Harvey/FPG International; p.14 ©Kugler, Jean/FPG International;
p.15 ©Travelpix/FPG International; p.16 ©Paul A. Sonders/CORBIS; p.17 ©Michaels,
Christian/FPG International; p.19 ©Shinichi Kanno/FPG International; p.21 ©David
Austen/FPG International; p.23 ©Patrick Ward/CORBIS; p.25 ©Rick Rycroft/AP/Wide World,
Inc.; p.27 ©Roger Ressmeyer/CORBIS; p.28a ©Travelpix/FPG International; p.28b ©Telegraph
Colour Library/FPG International; p.29a ©Travelpix/FPG International; p.29b ©David
Austen/FPG International.

All statistics in the Quick Facts section come from *The New York Times Almanac* (2000)
and *The World Almanac* (2000).

Contents

This Is Australia

The country of Australia is an island. In fact, it is the largest island in the world. Australia is also one of the world's seven continents, or great landmasses.

If you took your camera to Australia, you could take photographs of many things.

Perth is the largest city on Australia's west coast. Much of the country's wheat is grown on land near Perth.

In Australia's countryside, you might see large ranches where sheep and cattle are raised. You may even see koalas eating the leaves of eucalyptus, or gum, trees.

Australia has many large cities. One of them is Melbourne. This is Australia's second largest city. It is known for its skyscrapers and also for its lovely city parks.

This book will show you some of these places. It will also tell you much about Australia. If you learn about Australia before you take your camera there, you will enjoy your visit more.

Koalas are just one of many animals found only in Australia.

5 📷

The Place

Australia is the smallest continent. But it is a huge country. It is nearly 2,000 miles (3,220 km) from north to south and about 2,400 miles (3,860 km) from east to west. Australia is about the size of the United States.

Australia is far away from most other places. It takes more than a day to fly to the city of Sydney from New York City. Australia is so far south that sometimes it is referred to as Down Under. Because Australia is an island, it is completely surrounded by water. The Timor and Arafura seas are on the north. The Coral Sea is on the northeast. The eastern part of Australia touches the Pacific Ocean, and on the south and west is the Indian Ocean. Australia's coastline is 16,010 miles (25,760 km). The nearest landmass is Papua New Guinea.

Tasmania is a small island off Australia's south coast. It is part of Australia.

Arafura Sea

Timor Sea

Coral
Sea

n Ocean

Great Barrier Reef

Great Dividing Range

Alice Springs
Ayers Rock

Perth

New South Wales

Sydney
Canberra

Pacific Ocea

Melbourne

N

Indian Ocean

500 km

0   500 Miles

Tasmania

Most of Australia is flat, with many deserts.

Australia has one mountain range, the Great Dividing Range. It stretches down the eastern side of the country from north to south. The highest mountain is Mt. Kosciusko. It is 7,316 feet (2,230 m) high.

Because Australia is below the equator, the seasons are the reverse of those above it. Summer in Australia is from December to February, and winter is from June to August.

It is very hot in the north, but milder in the south. Near the equator temperatures of 100 degrees F (37 degrees C) have been recorded.

In Australia some cattle ranches cover thousands of square miles.

Bondi Beach is a very popular beach located near Sydney.

The north and northeast coasts are the wettest, with 40 to 80 inches (100 to 200 cm) of rain a year. In Sydney the rainfall is about 40 inches (100 cm) a year. In the deserts, there may be as little as 6 inches (15 cm) of rain a year, but in many years there may be no rain at all. Australia has many wind storms, dust storms, and cyclones every year. Cyclones are very strong windstorms.

9

Sydney

Sydney is Australia's oldest, largest, and most important city. It is the capital of a section of Australia known as New South Wales. Sydney was first settled in 1788.

Sydney has one of the best harbors in the world. It is also a busy one. Sydney has two famous landmarks, or sights. One of these is the Sydney Harbor Bridge. It was built in 1932 and is 1,650 feet (503 m) long. The

other famous sight is the Sydney Opera House, which was completed in 1973. Its wings have come to stand for Australians reaching into the future.

People who live in Sydney and its nearby suburbs use trains and buses to get to work every day. But because Sydney is near so much water, commuters also use fast boats and ferries for their daily commute. Like most modern cities, Sydney can have plenty of traffic jams during the daily rush hours. Most people who live in Sydney work in the manufacturing and tourist industries.

Botany Bay is near Sydney. An English explorer named Captain James Cook landed there in 1770. So many kinds of plants and flowers were growing there that one of his crew named the bay "Botany." Today it is part of Sydney's suburbs.

Sydney Harbor at night with two of Australia's best-known landmarks: the Sydney Opera House and behind it the Sydney Harbor Bridge.

Places to Visit

The Great Barrier Reef is the world's largest coral reef. A reef is a chain of coral near the surface of the water. The Great Barrier Reef is located near the northeast coast of Australia. It is made up of about 500 small islands and coral reefs. About 400 types of coral and 1,500 types of fish live in the clear warm water.

People come to the Great Barrier Reef to swim and snorkel so they can watch the rich wildlife.

Uluru is important to Australia's native people. It is also known as Ayers Rock.

One of Australia's most famous landmarks is Uluru. It is also known as Ayers Rock. It is a great red slab of rock that rises about 1,100 feet (335 m) from the flat desert in central Australia. Parts of the rock and its caves are decorated with drawings that are very old. The people drew graceful images of animals in charcoal and then colored them with chalk and clay.

Alice Springs is about 280 miles (450 km) northeast of Uluru. It is a town almost in the center of the country. Visitors go there because it looks almost like it did when it was first settled about 150 years ago.

13 📷

The People

Fewer people live in Australia than in most countries as large. About 19 million people live there. Almost all of them have ancestors who came from other countries, starting about 200 years ago. About 92 percent are Europeans, or have European ancestors. The first Europeans to settle in Australia were from Great Britain. About 7 percent of Australians today are Asian.

An even smaller number are Aborigines. This is the name early European settlers gave to the native people

The Aborigines have been in Australia for more than 40,000 years.

who were already living in Australia. The word *Aborigine* means "from the beginning." For many years these people were nomads. This means they wandered from place to place. When European settlers came, they took land away from the Aborigines. Recent laws have been passed that give the Aborigines more rights to the land.

The first Europeans who came to Australia settled throughout much of the country.

15 📷

Life in Australia

Most Australians live in cities. In cities, some Australians live in apartments, but most people like to live in houses. Three-fourths of Australians own their own homes. Many of the houses have small gardens. Some also have verandas and swimming pools. New suburbs surround the larger cities. Most Australian cities have skyscrapers. Because Australia is a fairly new country, there are very few old buildings.

Some Australians live on ranches, or stations. Often stations are far from one another. In fact, the distances are often so great between places in Australia that doctors use helicopters and small planes to see patients.

Most people in Australia live near the country's coasts. The outback and the bush begin away from the coast, in the interior. Outback is the name given to those parts of Australia that are isolated and rural. The bush is the area in Australia that has trees and woods. Even today there are few roads in much of the center of Australia. There are also areas there that have never been fully explored.

The kangaroo is world famous.

Many people like Australia's unique animal and plant life. One unusual animal that lives only in Australia is the kangaroo. It is world famous. But in some areas there are too many kangaroos so people have to hunt them.

Computers and good telephone systems make distances between sheep and cattle stations seem smaller.

17

Government and Religion

Australia has a democratic federal government. "Democratic" means that Australia's leaders are elected. "Federal" means that Australia is made up of a group of separate states that have joined together under one government. The country is made up of six states and two territories. Queen Elizabeth II of Great Britain is the official head of state, but she does not play any part in Australian politics. The queen's representative in Australia is called the governor-general. The prime minister is the real head of government. He or she is elected by the citizens of Australia.

Canberra is the capital of Australia. It is a small city that is part of the Australian Capital Territory. Like Washington, D.C., Canberra was created specially to be Australia's capital city.

Government buildings in Canberra

Most of Australia's people are Christians. About one half of them are Protestant and about one quarter are Roman Catholics. Roman Catholics are the most active, and attend weekly services. Most Roman Catholics send their children to religious schools.

There are some Jews and Muslims. Muslims follow the teachings of Mohammed. Their religion is called Islam.

Earning a Living

Australia is large and still growing, so there are plenty of jobs for many people.

Because the land is so dry, only about 10 percent of it can be used for farming. Wheat, barley, oats, and sugarcane are grown. Grapes, corn, and other fruits and vegetables are also grown. But only about 5 percent of Australia's workers are farmers.

Instead, raising cattle, sheep, and pigs is very important to the Australian economy. About 30 percent of the world's supply of wool comes from Australia's sheep. Beef, lamb, wool, and wheat are Australia's chief exports, or goods that are sent out of the country to be sold in another.

Australia's main industries are iron, steel, cloth, electrical equipment, chemicals, and machinery. Making cars, aircraft, and ships is also important. Australia's natural resources include coal, copper, iron, lead, tin, uranium, and zinc. Gold, diamonds, and opals are among the country's more valuable resources. Oil and natural gas are important industries. They continue to grow larger from year to year.

Many people come to Australia for long visits. They are eager to see some of Australia's unique animal and plant life. As a result, tourism is growing each year. About one third of Australians work in the tourist industry.

Mining is an important industry in Australia.

School and Sports

Children in Australia have to go to school between the ages of 6 and 15. In out-of-the-way areas, children may get their lessons from the School of the Air.

Teachers teach their classes by two-way radio. Students ask their questions and teachers answer them by radio. In this way teachers can reach students spread out over hundreds of square miles.

There are more than 20 universities in Australia, including Sydney University and Melbourne University.

Because Australia has a warm and sunny climate, outdoor sports are extremely popular. Some sports came with settlers from Great Britain many years ago and are still popular. Cricket, rugby, and golf are among these. Australians who live near the coast especially like to go swimming and surfing. Many people enjoy hunting and fishing.

Water sports are very popular along Australia's coasts.

Food and Holidays

Much of the cooking in Australia is based on the dishes brought by the first settlers from Great Britain. Australians eat a lot of beef and lamb. This is because Australians raise so many cattle and sheep. Like many people around the world, however, Australians are cutting back on the amount of red meat they eat. More and more people are eating fresh vegetables and fruits.

Australians are outdoors people, and they enjoy barbecues. They like to set up their grills and cook steaks. They also like to dine out at many of the larger cities' fine restaurants. More recent peoples who have come to Australia, such as Asians, have brought their own foods and recipes to the country.

As in Great Britain, Christmas and Boxing Day are the most important holidays. Boxing Day is on

Some Australians hold Christmas parties on the beach.

December 26, the day after Christmas. At one time families gave "boxes" of money and small gifts to servants and storekeepers on this day. Because Christmas comes during Australia's summer, Australians think of this holiday in terms of warm sunshine and growing flowers. Easter comes in Australia's autumn.

25 📷

The Future

Because Australia is a fairly new country, there is room for much growth. Modern technology is ideal for helping Australia develop. Telephones, faxes, computers and especially the Internet and e-mail solve the problems of great distances in this huge country.

Like many large countries, Australia has some problems. Although there a lot of jobs for people, the jobs seem to be part-time ones. But there is little crime and very little pollution. Also, Australians are proud of their many unique plants and animals and are taking care to protect them. The people have set aside many national parks and animal preserves.

The future will bring more understanding of the Aborigines. This will lead to a greater appreciation of their ancient culture, which is one of the world's oldest.

A typical Australian greeting is "Good day, mate." With the Australian accent, it sounds more like "G-day, might."

Modern technology helps Australians keep in touch with one another and the rest of the world.

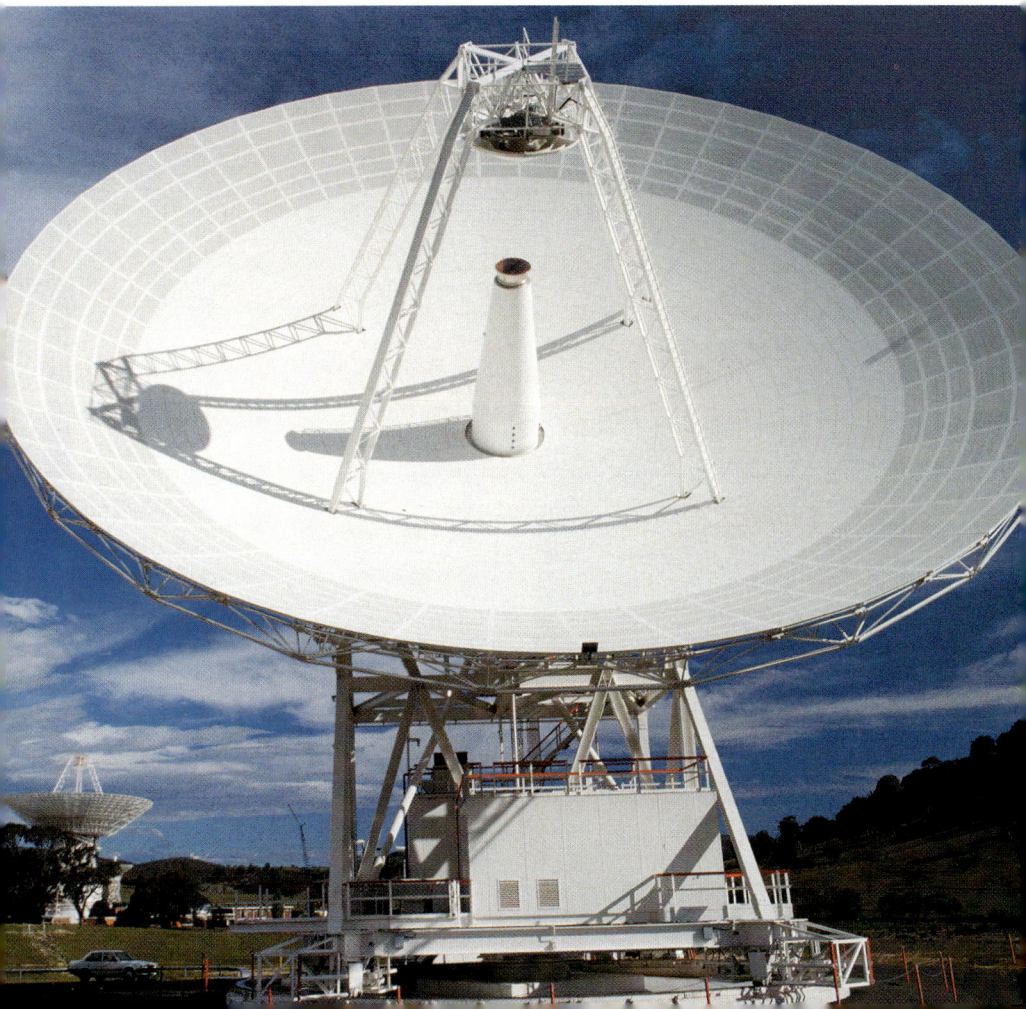

Quick Facts About
AUSTRALIA

Capital
Canberra

Borders
Indian Ocean
Pacific Ocean

Area
2,967,897 square miles
(7,686,850 sq km)

Population
18.8 million

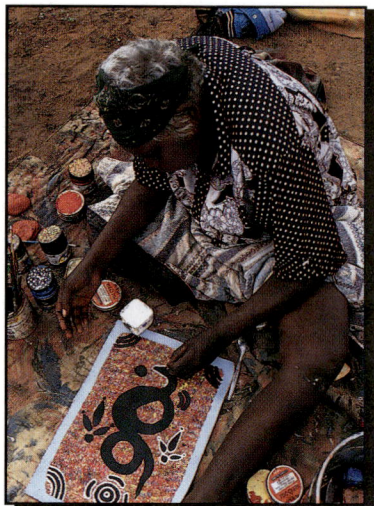

Largest cities
Canberra (325,400 people);
Sydney (3,719,000 people);
Melbourne (3,187,500 people)

Chief crops
wheat, barley, sugarcane, fruits,
poultry

Natural resources
bauxite, coal, iron ore, copper, tin

Longest river
Murray, at 1,609 miles (2,589 km)

Flag of Australia

◀ **Coastline**
16,010 miles (25,760 km)

Monetary unit
Australian dollar

Literacy rate
100 percent of the Australians can read and write.

Major industries
mining, industrial and transportation equipment, food processing

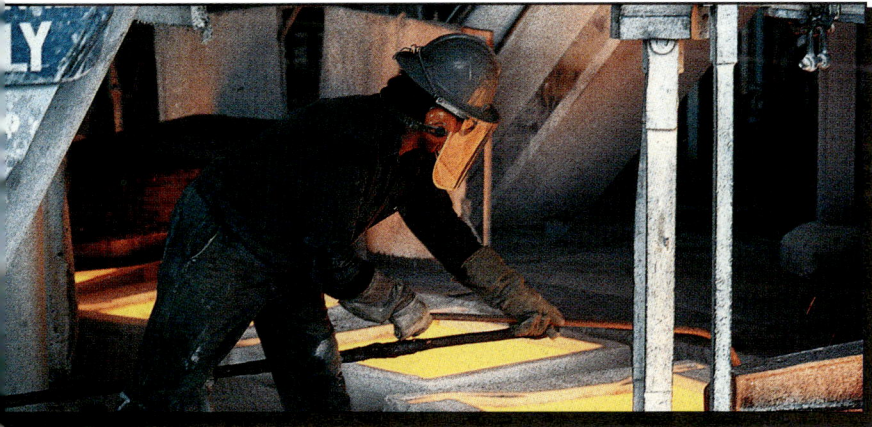

Glossary

Aborigines (ah-buh-RIJ-neez) The native people who were living in Australia for perhaps 40,000 years. The word means "from the beginning."

Ayers Rock (ARZ) A great red slab of rock that rises from the desert floor and is one of Australia's most famous landmarks. It is also called Uluru.

bush The area in Australia that has trees and woods

Canberra (KAN-ber-uh) The capital of Australia

continent (KONT-nunt) One of Earth's seven huge landmasses

coral reef A reef made of coral and other materials that have hardened into rock

cyclones (SEYE-klownz) Large windstorms

Down Under Another name for Australia

equator (ee-KWAY-tur) The imaginary line around the center of the Earth that divides it into two equal parts

exports Goods that are sent out of the country to be sold in another country

governor-general The British queen's representative in Australia

Great Barrier Reef The world's largest coral reef, which is made up of 500 small islands and coral reefs

Islam (is-LAHM) The religion begun by Mohammed

Melbourne (MEL-burn) Australia's second largest city

Muslims (MUHZ-luhm) People who follow the teachings of Mohammed

natural resources Things from nature that are useful to people

nomads People who wander from place to place

outback The name given to those parts of Australia that are isolated and rural

Perth (PURTH) The largest city on Australia's west coast

reef A chain of coral near the surface of the water

School of the Air Classes that use two-way radios to teach children who live in out-of-the-way areas in Australia

stations The Australian word for ranch

Sydney (SID-nee) Australia's oldest, largest, and most important city, and the capital of New South Wales

Uluru (oo-LOO-roo) The Aborigine name for Ayers Rock

31

Index